Let Us Go Back!

Frank H. Keith

Let us go back to the beauties
  That are pocketed deep in our past--
The joys we relinquished with childhood
  But which hauntingly linger and last!

Let us return to the Christmas
  That remains with the children of time--
The Christmas of wonderful wishes,
  Of stardust, and snowdrift, and chime!

Let us go back to the vision
  Of evergreen peace in our rooms,
Gay ribbons on gifts of the giving,
  And the Dream that consistently blooms.

Let us in piety wander
  Where the veil of the centuries parts
To look at a Crib and an Infant,
  And Christmas will live in our hearts!

CHRISTMAS MEMORY LANE

editor
van b. hooper

Christmas Fifty Years Ago

Ellen N. Youtz

Remember the bridge the reindeer crossed,
On the frozen river's banks,
And the clumpity-clump of stomping hoofs
Resounding on old planks?
We huddled beneath the patchwork quilt
Lest each breath turn to frost,
Or peeked around the stove-pipe hole
Afraid old Nick was lost!

Remember how reindeer horns would lock
In nightmare's shadowland,
And the positive way he'd jerk the reins
Which caused each deer to stand
At our own door! Oh jimin-ee —
We thought our heart would burst,
Then out would tumble fat, old Nick
With our own presents first!

Remember the way *he'd* sneak inside
Without a trace or a track,
And the sneaky way your cold, cold feet
Would find my good, warm back?
And, ugh! the frost on the window panes
Where finger nails would write
The things we wanted old Saint Nick
To bring that Christmas night!

Remember how far we heard sleigh bells
Come jingling up Hall's Run?
Remember that inside balky deer —
He was a son-of-a-gun!
Closer, closer the jingle came
Then, we ducked our heads,
And slithered off to slide in Nod
On a pair of old bob sleds!

The old plank bridge the reindeer crossed
Is flashed by memory now,
It played its part to transfer man
And horse and brindled cow;
Its old stone piers are washed away,
Long gone its trusty ties,
And old Nick's reindeer now must cross
On memory's bridge of sighs!

Christmas... and Snowbound, In the Treasured Past

by Erwin L. Hess

We remember our best Christmas. A flashback appears and this favorite Christmas plays on a very special screen in a picture of color, and we see the scenes we remember so well. Immediately our story we'll begin to tell.... It snowed early that year. In those days the holiday spirit was in the air with the first fall of snow. Sleighbells jingled and that meant Christmas was near!

Christmastime was simpler than the glamorous ones of later days — but richer. We had the pleasure of living amidst those colorful old scenes, like the pictures that now are morseled out to folks on greeting cards. With the feeling of nostalgia, we continue our story, abundant with memories....

We were smalltown folks, and.... Papa and another nice, easygoing man owned the general store. In those days Christmastime was an old-fashioned, homemade holiday season. Most folks made things which turned out to be gifts....and they loved making them. Those were the days of simplicity, yet satisfyingly pleasant golden days of long ago.....

There were no Christmas trees for sale on city lots in those days but there were many trees to choose from. A walk in the cold, crisp air to some small woods, a sharpened ax in hand and we had one! That year Papa picked out a great big, beautiful tree!

The big tree was set up in the unheated front room, generally closed up for the winter. All week before Christmas, Mamma confined herself mostly to the holiday kitchen, baking cookies. And as the days went by, we began to burst with anxiety, knowing that the night 'fore Christmas was approaching and Santa Claus was very near. Finally Christmas Eve arrived....

The lamplighter came early on that Christmas Eve. Lights from windows glinted yellow and orange on the snow. Sleighs glided through the blueness of the night and out in the distant darkness, every so often a light from a lantern flickered. Townsfolk moved along the snowy streets to the church. We were among them. The night was filled with enchantment and it was ablaze with the Christmas spirit of old. It was beautiful, so perfectly pretty....

It was the beginning of our best Christmas. In the morning we would drive 'way out in the country to visit Grandpa and Grandma. Later that night Papa filled the bottom of the bobsled with hay. The light from the kerosene lantern glowed like gold paint on the hay. Out in the frosty air, we watched him...

When we went into the house, the parlor door was open and there was our big tree, lighted by little wax candles that twinkled like stars on every tip and twig. A maze of glow and glitter had changed the front room into a fairyland, and Santa Claus had been there early.....

At first we stood spellbound, as if entangled in a web of fascination. But, then with a scream of delight, we bounded out of our state of bewilderment and we re-entered the land of reality, and we touched the toys and the other gifts. Incredible happiness was heaped upon us, and it flowed over us and it danced around us. We bubbled over with joy and then, much too soon, bedtime came.

We said our prayers, we were tucked in bed, Mamma's
goodnight kiss followed and the lamp was put out. The
door was open and after watching the glow from the
heater and listening to the jingling of sleighbells out in
the frosty air, we slowly drifted into slumberland. It was
not easy to fall asleep, but the sandman came, too, on
that Christmas Eve. He knew that we had to get up
early on Christmas Day for the ride out to the country.

Christmas morning sparkled. A tinsel of snow whirled in the air. Up early, we
ran to our toys and touched them fondly until Mamma called from the kitchen,
"Get dressed. Breakfast's ready!" Soon we were in the bobsled, all bundled up,
snuggled deep down in the hay, old quilts over us and hot flatirons at our feet.
The drive 'way out in the country began. It was pretty out there. As far as our
eyes could see, there were miles of snow — a dazzling wonderland of whiteness.

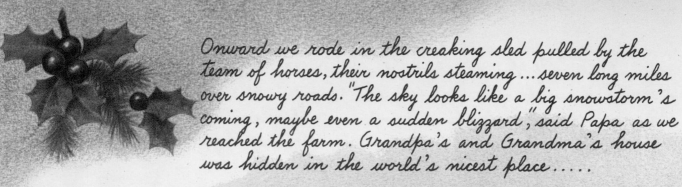

Onward we rode in the creaking sled pulled by the team of horses, their nostrils steaming...seven long miles over snowy roads. "The sky looks like a big snowstorm's coming, maybe even a sudden blizzard", said Papa as we reached the farm. Grandpa's and Grandma's house was hidden in the world's nicest place.....

It seemed to be tucked away in some far-off land of silence, peace and contentment. It was a wonderland, wrapped in snow on Christmas Day.

Grandpa and Grandma welcomed us in their usual, sincere manner. At their house the Christmas spirit prevailed all year 'round. We stomped into the warm kitchen and its savory smells of cooking made us hungrier than ever. Mamma put on an apron to help Grandma with the forthcoming dinner and the kitchen vibrated with holiday happiness. Grandma kept vigil at the oven. The turkey was coming to a crusty, golden brown.....

And then we ate that wholesome, old-fashioned Christmas dinner. After we finished, the grownups settled down to more conversation and to exchanging gifts. Among the ones for us, Grandma had made red mittens and Grandpa had made a sled. He even had a blacksmith put iron runners on it. In the afternoon a sudden snowstorm struck! Papa had been right. Grandpa looked out the window often and as evening came, he said, "It's turning into a blizzard. We're going to be snowbound!" It sounded so exciting!

We remember that night so well;
a raging blizzard outside.....

And we remember how nice it was
to be snowbound 'way out in that
nicest place in the world.... and on
Christmas night, too! And we recall
how Grandpa recited the poem by
James Whitcomb Riley.....

" Winter without
        And warmth within:
The winds may shout
        And the storm begin
While here in my room
        I'm as snugly shut
As a glad little worm
        In the heart of a nut!"

'twas exactly how we felt...

It was a lamplighted night to remember, such a nice ending for a holiday
season which was destined to become our best Christmas. As we departed for
home several days later, all the gladnesses that had piled up seemed to warm
us in the crisp, stinging air. We can never go back again, except in our recollections.
Now, with a stockpile of memories stored up, we can always see a repeat
showing of an old favorite, "Christmas...and Snowbound, in the Treasured Past."

Christmas Meditation

Frank Carleton Nelson

As tonight I sit in silence
  with my eyes upon the tree,
And ponder on the favors
  that the world has given me
Throughout the year now ending,
  I am simply forced to say
I am all the while receiving,
  but it seems I seldom pay,
When I strike a balance on it,
  I am willing to confess,
I have failed to make a payment
  on the year of happiness,
And I cannot help but wonder
  if I'm doing what is right,
As I set and think it over
  by the Christmas tree tonight.

Yes, I'm all the while receiving,
  but it seems, I seldom give,
And I cannot help but wonder
  if it's just the way to live,
It's vain to think I'm paying
  for the good things given me
By the inexpensive presents
  I have placed upon the tree,
I have tried to do subtracting,
  I have tried addition, too,
I've multiplied, divided,
  but, I find the debt is due,
A debt that I am owing
  and it's one that hurts my pride,
A debt that I'm confessing,
  for it's one I cannot hide.

Lord, grant me this one favor,
  in the year that is before,
May I do a little better,
  may I give a little more,
May I add a little something
  to the world that's helping me,
May I come a little nearer
  to the man I ought to be.
Oh, it's not a case of giving,
  only paying what is due,
And I long to help a little,
  as the year I journey through,
Lord, grant me this, I ask it
  from the bottom of my heart,
For the favors I'm receiving,
  may I pay at least a part.

An Old Fashioned Christmas

Adam N. Reiter

Away with a dash and jingling bells,
   In a two-horse cutter sleigh,
The children are off to Grandmother's house,
   For an old-style Christmas Day.
There's sparkling beauty o'er valley and hill,
   And a nip in the frosty air;
There's hearty cheer in the neighbor's hail,
   And gladness everywhere.

A grand old place is Grandmother's house,
   Massive and rambling and low,
Nestled and hid in the lee of a hill,
   And wrapped in a blanket of snow.
Down the lane and over the bridge,
   Then on to the opened door;
Greeted by Rover's welcome bark,
   And those who've arrived before.

Grandmother's kitchen is all aglow
   With a friendly cheer of its own,
With singing kettle and glowing hearth,
   That beams with the warmth of home.
Grandfather sits in his easy chair
   With his favorite pipe alight;
The clan has gathered — the children are home —
   It's Christmas and "all is right!"

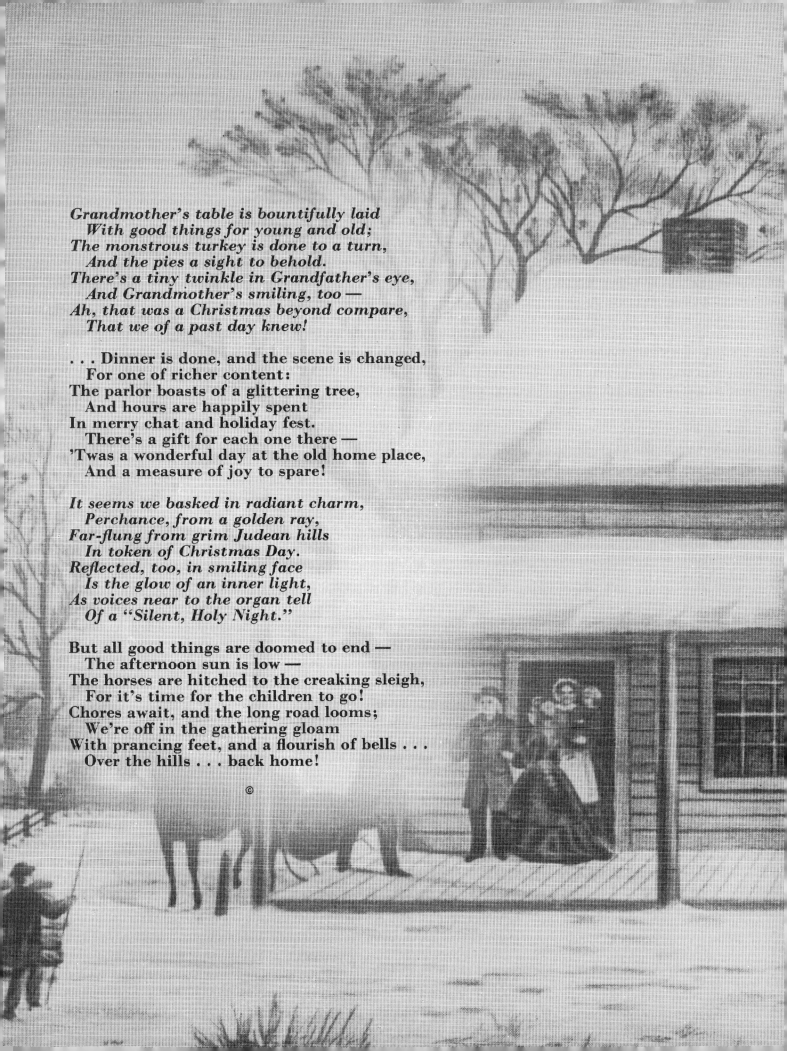

Grandmother's table is bountifully laid
  With good things for young and old;
The monstrous turkey is done to a turn,
  And the pies a sight to behold.
There's a tiny twinkle in Grandfather's eye,
  And Grandmother's smiling, too —
Ah, that was a Christmas beyond compare,
  That we of a past day knew!

. . . Dinner is done, and the scene is changed,
  For one of richer content:
The parlor boasts of a glittering tree,
  And hours are happily spent
In merry chat and holiday fest.
  There's a gift for each one there —
'Twas a wonderful day at the old home place,
  And a measure of joy to spare!

It seems we basked in radiant charm,
  Perchance, from a golden ray,
Far-flung from grim Judean hills
  In token of Christmas Day.
Reflected, too, in smiling face
  Is the glow of an inner light,
As voices near to the organ tell
  Of a "Silent, Holy Night."

But all good things are doomed to end —
  The afternoon sun is low —
The horses are hitched to the creaking sleigh,
  For it's time for the children to go!
Chores await, and the long road looms;
  We're off in the gathering gloam
With prancing feet, and a flourish of bells . . .
  Over the hills . . . back home!

Snowman

Virginia Pennock

The kids have built a snowman,
I wish that you could see.
He stands outside our door
  and winks,
As brazen as can be.

He wears a topper grandly;
He carries grandpa's cane;
He even sports a muffler
That once belonged to Jane.

He waves at all the neighbors.
O, he has friends galore —
Our made to measure snowman
Beside our kitchen door.

I wish I were a snowman . . .
You indicate surprise —
You know I've always wanted
Those sparkling coal black eyes.

The Ring of the Skates

R. H. Sotherland

A moonlight winding river
Covered o'er with crystal ice,
Outlined by knarled old sycamores,
A picture without price.
Skaters winding here and there,
Graceful in their flight,
A boy and girl floating by
Sweethearts of the night.

Ring of steel as the skates cut through,
Leaving a feather edge of frost,
A great bonfire on the river bank,
Its flames in darkness lost.
Calls and laughter of the youngsters
As they do the figure eight,
A snirling dancing dervish,
Attracting attention by his gait.

Chosen sides in a game of shinny,
The roots of the hickory trees,
Clubs used to play the game,
No use for golfer's tees.
Then away up the glistening river,
To a little island shack,
Where a fire roars up a chimney
To enjoy a little snack.

Then back again to the starting place,
Your being all aglow,
The tingling bite of a winter night,
The trudge back home through the snow.
Then into your bed for a good night's rest,
The shinny club and the skates on the floor
Your clothes thrown over the back of a chair,
Wouldn't you like to do it once more?

Christmas Shopping After School

Grace Noll Crowell

With five in a family — a quarter to spend —
There was never a happier child than I,
As I trudged to town on a snowy day
For the beautiful things that my money would buy.

*The silver coins in my mittened palm;
The snow flakes white on my crimson hood.
And in my breast an excited heart
Fluttered as any glad thing would.*

And there was the shop down the little street,
The quaintest shop that you ever could see,
Where a jovial man, and his rosy wife,
Were the smiling merchants who welcomed me:

*A small, eager girl with snow in her eyes,
Half blind with the glitter of tinsel that hung
From ceiling to counter, from window to door,
With baubles that glinted and glittered and swung.*

A glorious counter to linger beside,
And every decision a momentous thing:
A doll, or a jew's harp, a flower-sprigged mug,
Or a whirl-i-gig top that danced on a string?

*Small gifts with the heart of the giver thrown in,
All purchased and wrapped to the last splendid one,
And with five packages under my arms,
My feet would trudge homeward, my gay shopping done.*

O dear little girl, going back through the dusk,
To home, to a window, a lamp shining through,
I could cry for the things that the long years have lost —
How I wish I could shop again, some day with you.

©

A Letter to Santy

Author Unknown

"I'll give you a pointer, Willy,"
Said Tommie, the other day.
If you want certain things at Christmas
You'd better try my way.

It's easy and very simple,
And always works, for I
Have tried it many and many a time
At Christmases gone by.

Write Santa Claus a letter
In your very bestest hand,
And give him a list of things you want
Don't matter at all, how grand.

And then when the letter is written,
Just take it to dear old dad,
And ask if he thinks the spelling
And writing is awful bad.

I once wrote a letter to Santy,
And sent it off right away.
And not a thing I asked for
Was sent on Christmas Day.

But the letter I showed to Daddy,
To see if it was written right,
Brought everything I wanted
The following Christmas night.

I don't know just how he knew it,
But pa knows a thing or two,
About how old Santa should be addressed,
By children like me and you.

From the personal scrapbook of
Mrs. Gleta Smith, Constantine, Michigan.

As Fine A Friend As You

Albert Kennedy Rowswell

At Christmas time when joy bells ring
And hearts are light and gay,
We turn the pages back again
For just one fleeting day.

And there the friends of yesteryear
Pass by in swift review —
It's something to have lived and known
As fine a friend as you.

Sometimes the skies have been o'ercast
The sun refused to shine;
Sometimes the road has weary been
And hope was on decline;

But always came the cheering thought
And courage would renew —
It's something to have lived and known
As fine a friend as you.

At Christmas time when hearts rejoice
And all the world seems fair —
When selfishness is put aside,
We've happiness to share;

May fortune smile on you and yours
And light your path anew —
It's something to have lived and known
As fine a friend as you.

O Christmas is a time for love,
    A time for tender giving;
A time for faith and hope and cheer,
    A time for sweeter living.

A time to reach across the world,
    Or just across the street;
A time to send good will afar,
    Or give to those you meet.

And so I send you faith and hope,
    Good will and wishes true;
And add a special bit of love
    I've saved for only you.

Letitia Morse Nash

*Copyrighted. Used by
permission of Arthur M. Nash.*

Christmas Wants

W. Waldemar Argow

What do you want for Christmas? Of a truth, the answer to no other question so completely serves as an index of what we are at heart. At other times of the year we can pretend and make believe, but at Christmastime our true nature reveals itself and we act from the hidden motives that dominate our lives.

Come with me this Yuletide and let the heart express those wishes it has ever longed for, but never dared express! Aye, what is it we want?

I want a few sincere friends, who understand my loneliness, yet remain loyal when I am silent.

I want a growing capacity to understand and respond to the un-uttered sufferings of others, knowing that they fight as hard a battle against many odds, even as I.

I want a sense of duty tempered with beauty; a conception of work as a privilege, an urge to justice mingled with mercy, and a feeling that responsibility is my debt for the opportunity of living in a day when great aims are at stake.

I want a task to do which has abiding value, without which the lives of men would be poorer, and the good I might do be eternally lost.

I want a sense of humor, and the genius to laugh; the grace to forgive; and the humility to be forgiven, the willingness to praise, and the freedom to enjoy a little leisure with tantalizing dreams.

I want a glimpse of kneeling hillsides, the unresting sea, the horizon-enchanting plains, and the thrill of a few high-tangled bird notes keenly thinned.

I want a few wistful moments of quiet amid the garish noises and fevered fret of the day; and when twilight flecks the eventide with spotted shadows, a sense of the presence of God.

The More The Years

Douglas Malloch

The more the years the more we all remember
Our yesterdays, the things that used to be,
The summertime seems fairer in December,
And roses fade, but not from memory.
Youth has so much, and thinks how empty age is,
With only dreams of things so long ago,
But we who sit and turn life's lovely pages,
What joy we know!

The more the years the more our sorrows soften,
The more the years the more they turn to gold,
Yes, life's a tale, though told however often,
That fairer grows with ev'ry time it's told.
Youth has today, and youth is young and clever,
Age only yesterdays of smiles and tears,
And yet the past grows lovelier forever,
The more the years.

In Lowly Places

Mrs. Roy L. Peifer

Sometimes in the lowliest places
The most wondrous of treasures are found,
The most brilliant and precious diamonds
Buried deep in the blackest ground.

'Twas a strange place to seek for a King —
In a stable, lowly and bare —
But shepherds from Judean hills
Found the little Lord Jesus there.

©

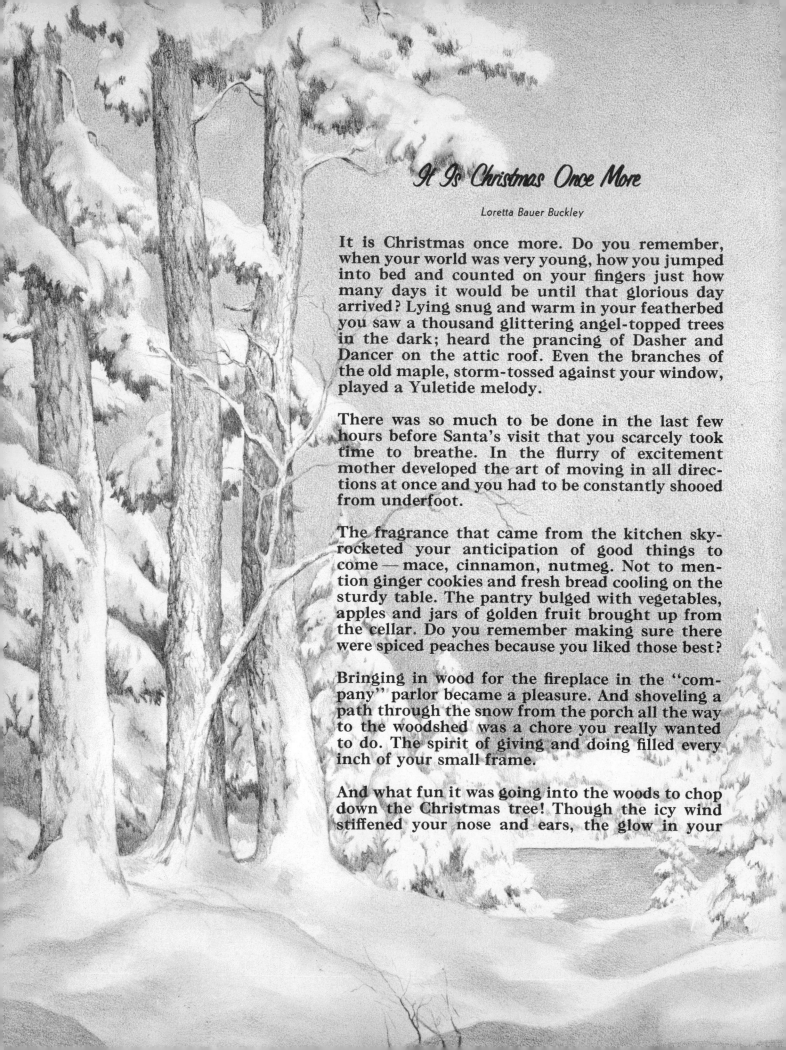

It Is Christmas Once More

Loretta Bauer Buckley

It is Christmas once more. Do you remember, when your world was very young, how you jumped into bed and counted on your fingers just how many days it would be until that glorious day arrived? Lying snug and warm in your featherbed you saw a thousand glittering angel-topped trees in the dark; heard the prancing of Dasher and Dancer on the attic roof. Even the branches of the old maple, storm-tossed against your window, played a Yuletide melody.

There was so much to be done in the last few hours before Santa's visit that you scarcely took time to breathe. In the flurry of excitement mother developed the art of moving in all directions at once and you had to be constantly shooed from underfoot.

The fragrance that came from the kitchen sky-rocketed your anticipation of good things to come — mace, cinnamon, nutmeg. Not to mention ginger cookies and fresh bread cooling on the sturdy table. The pantry bulged with vegetables, apples and jars of golden fruit brought up from the cellar. Do you remember making sure there were spiced peaches because you liked those best?

Bringing in wood for the fireplace in the "company" parlor became a pleasure. And shoveling a path through the snow from the porch all the way to the woodshed was a chore you really wanted to do. The spirit of giving and doing filled every inch of your small frame.

And what fun it was going into the woods to chop down the Christmas tree! Though the icy wind stiffened your nose and ears, the glow in your

heart more than made up for the pain you knew. As the tree was placed in the barn, you were certain you heard a baby's cry come from the hayloft. You had prepared a crib — and did not miracles happen at Christmastide? Frankincense and myrrh were strange-sounding gifts, so you left part of a nameless joy you felt there beside the small manger. . .

Once in the parlor the redolence of the tall fir, as the warmth of the room touched it, cast a perfume you said you would never forget. And you promised to remember always the ruby red cranberry chains that swung gayly from its emerald branches.

The ritual of hanging your stocking was one that shattered your heart into diamond-like fragments of happiness. You could never find a word for that enchanted moment — even to this day. Then to bed, and 'though the floor was as cold as the pond on which you hoped to try your new skates, you did not leave out a single prayer. The first one was for the Baby Jesus, and the last for the safety of Saint Nicholas.

The eve of Christmas is upon us once again. Candles of memory flame brightly over the years and the miles of drifted snow. In your dreams tonight may you hear the cry of the New Born King as you heard it in childhood's golden hours; songs of herald angels; shepherds' sandaled steps on Bethlehem's starlit road. And may you wake to a world grown miraculously new, beautiful beyond belief, because a Little Child came into it with the gift of perfect love for all men.

©

The Buying of Gifts

Grace Noll Crowell

When I was a child on my father's farm,
And Christmastime drew near,
I would trudge thru the snow to the little town . . .
Oh, the memory is quite clear
Of the little girl with a quarter to spend
For parents, for brother, and sister, and friend.

My scarlet mittens and scarlet hood
Were white with glistening snow,
My eyes were shining with eagerness,
My frost-bright cheeks aglow,
As I went gladly, hurrying down
To the novelty store in the little town.

And oh, the rapture, the sheer delight!
The shop's small windows shone
With beautiful things . . . and there was I
With a quarter all my own!
I searched — and will wonders never cease?
I found five gifts for a nickel apiece.

Such beautiful gifts! And trudging home
Thru the winter dusk, I knew
A joy and a glowing happiness
That has lasted the long years thru.
For something of that far Christmastime
Stayed in my heart and it still is mine.

©

Only A Little Town

Esther Baldwin York

On all the other nights it had been only a little town, half-hidden in the darkness.

Then came that Night of Nights when Light came to Bethlehem. There was the dazzling glory of the angel choir brightening the skies of the surrounding country. There was the pure white light of the Star that stood over a stable roof. There was the golden radiance emanating from the Baby in the manger, making beautiful the humble stable and everything in it. There was the light of happiness in Mary's eyes and the light of love and wonder in the eyes of all who came to behold the little Saviour.

Light travels fast and far. And the Light from Bethlehem still shines brightly today in the hearts of all who love Him.

©

No Calendar Needed

Lolita Pinney

For many years a calendar
  hung on our kitchen wall
And Mother checked the busy days
  and seasons as they'd fall,
But no calendar was needed
  to know the time of year:
By the fragrance of her kitchen,
  I knew the season near!

The aroma of hot chile
  when the wintry air was cold;
The rhubarb custards cooling
  when spring's magic would unfold;
Bubbling jellies in the kettle
  when the summer heat was high;
And in frosty, tangy autumn,
  whiffs of spicy pumpkin pie!

True, no calendar was needed
  for an eager child to know
That Christmas time was coming!
  Mother hurried to and fro

Making special sugar cookies
  and our maple sugar candy.
While she whistled Christmas carols,
  we knew everything was dandy!

Gingerbread men in the pantry
  and the fruitcake in the jar
Teased your nostrils every minute —
  oh, the day could not be far!
We cracked nutmeats on the flatiron,
  and strung popcorn for the tree
And every hour was heaven
  in the kitchen, seems to me!

Mother in her big white apron
  with some flour on her cheek
Is the dearest recollection
  of my cherished Christmas week;
A calendar was useless,
  but the essence was bewitchin'
And you always knew 'twas Christmas
  by the fragrance in the kitchen!

©

The Story Often Told...
But Still Forever New

Rose Cordain

"Mommy, why is there a star
Upon our Christmas tree,
And why is it so big and bright,
Please tell it all to me."

Each year a mother hears this question,
And then she must review
The story that's been often told,
But still forever new.

"Long, long ago in Palestine,
Upon a night serene,
A wondrous star flamed in the east,
The brightest ever seen.

And people wondered as they looked,
If this might be a sign,
That God would work a miracle
To show His hand divine.

And there were shepherds on a hill,
Who watched their flocks that night,
When suddenly the whole sky glowed
With a blinding, radiant light.

The shepherds were amazed and awed,
They shook with trembling fear,
Then slowly from the light they saw
An angel form appear.

'Fear not' he said, 'I bring you news
Of peace to be restored,
For unto you this day is born,
A Savior, Christ the Lord.'

The joyful shepherds left their flocks,
And started following
The shining star that would lead them
To see the newborn King.

And in another region were
Three Magi, old and wise,
They, too, looked on the gleaming star
But it brought them no surprise.

This was the sign long prophesied;
The day was now at hand,
When a great new King would come
To bring peace to the land.

The Magi gathered precious gifts
Of gold and spices sweet —
A tribute to the Savior Child,
And lay them at His feet.

They mounted camels and they wrapped
Their robes about them tight.
The shepherds too, trudged slowly on
Throughout the chilly night.

Before the wanderers went the star,
It stopped at Bethlehem,
And now they knew the miracle
Would be revealed to them.

About the city streets they searched
For a palace high and grand,
That would be fitting for a King
Who was to rule the land.

The star came down at last to rest,
Above a stable door,
The travelers saw animals,
And straw upon the floor.

'Where is the King that is to be?'
They asked in great surprise —
The donkeys and the cows and sheep,
Turned on them wondering eyes.

A man named Joseph greeted them,
His face was worn and thin,
'We have been quartered here' he said,
'No room was at the inn.

'And this is Mary, my dear wife,
So gentle, pure and mild,
We've travelled far from Nazareth,
Tonight was born the Child.'

He pointed to a manger crib,
And there upon the hay,
Surrounded by a radiance,
The Infant Jesus lay.

The Magi and the shepherds knew
That here was Christ the Lord —
They knelt upon the stable floor,
And worshipped and adored.

And it is said, the cattle knelt,
The sheep and donkeys too,
That God was in the tiny Babe,
In their dumb way they knew.

And high above the stable roof,
A host of angels sang,
'Glory to God in the highest,'
All night their voices rang.

And so each year we tell the tale,
Of Jesus' humble birth,
That men may live in brotherhood,
And peace be on the earth.

And then we put the shining star,
Upon the Christmas tree,
To show God's promise to the world,
And His love for you and me.''

Memory Clings To These

Edgar A. Guest

There used to be a sideboard,
  in the days when I was small,
Which with tasty things was loaded
  for the friends who came to call.
There were little pies of mincemeat
  and a plate of lemon tarts,
Which in England are the custom
  when the Christmas season starts.
There were almonds mixed with raisins;
  there was fruitcake, dark and light.
There were cookies for the children,
  always frosted red and white.

It is strange what memory clings to —
  The plum pudding always came
To the table decked with holly
  and for Christmas Day aflame.
With an apple in its mouth
  was a roasted suckling pig,
Which for mother's finest platter
  was a little bit too big.
And my father, I remember,
  seemed the happiest of men
As he stood to do the carving
  for his family back then.

Oh, the years are long and many
  since my parents went away,
But I always feel their presence
  very close on Christmas Day.
And I always see the sideboard
  with its pie and cookie trays,
And the almonds and the raisins
  and the pudding set ablaze.
I was just a little fellow,
  but tenaciously I hold
To the wonder and the gladness
  of those Christmas days of old.

An Old Fashioned Sleigh Ride

Anne Campbell

Remember the thrill of the old-fashioned sleigh ride,
The straw in the sleigh and the bells ringing clear,
The road stretching white and the moon shining o'er us,
A hand in our own that was clinging and dear?

Perhaps there were ten of us there in the party,
Five girls and five boys that we liked best of all,
We planned for a square-dancing sociable evening
And spelling down, too, at the old Wickham Hall.

Remember the thrill of the old-fashioned sleigh ride,
The stretch of the country o'er which we must go,
The meadows so white, and the houses so scattered,
The songs that we sang as we sped through the snow?

"Robin Adair," and "The Old Oaken Bucket,"
"Tenting Tonight," and "The Sweet By and By."
And all of us sang "When the Roll's Called Up Yonder,"
And smiled at the stars in the far-away sky.

Remember the thrill of the old-fashioned sleigh ride,
The lap robes of fur kept us cozy and warm;
The light in the window that beckoned us onward,
The hall when we reached it, its quaintness and charm?

Oh, talk as you like of our modern improvements,
Our autos are nice and their comfort is plain,
But oh, to be young in the beautiful country,
And ride in an old-fashioned sleigh once again!

©

To The Years That Used To Be

Annette Victorin

The shining, sparkling ornaments
Strung on our Christmas tree,
Reach out and take me by the hand
To years that used to be:

I am a little girl once more,
Our tree wears candlelights,
We sing the songs the angels sang
And thrill to simple sights.

A star tops our small Christmas tree,
Red apples hug each bough,
Long strings of popcorn and bright chains . . .
(If those days were here now!)

Grampa tells us of the Three Wise Men
Who came to Bethlehem,
I dream a little girlish dream
In which I follow them.

The shining, sparkling ornaments
Strung on our Christmas tree,
Reach out and take me by the hand
To years that used to be!

An Old Country Church

P. F. Freeman

There's an old country church 'way back in memory
That I never expect to visit again,
But I'll never forget it — the church in the valley
Where the old and the young for Christmas would rally.

There was always a tree and candles aglow
To cast a shadow on the glistening snow,
As a good old Santa dressed in his best
Would find a present for every guest.

I still seem to hear the bell that would ring,
And a message of good tidings its tolling would bring,
As in sleighs filled with straw and from miles around
Came gay country folks in answer to its sound.

'Twas there at the church that true friendships were born,
Surviving many holidays that have passed and gone,
As good folks joined together to frolic and play
And be happy and cheerful on a Christmas Day.

Christmas Time, Long, Long Ago

Jessy Mae Coker

Rolling hills and pigmy canyons knee-deep in soft, fluffy snow . . . nights radiant with pale light . . . sleigh rides . . . bells dancing on crisp, quiet air!

Weeks of dashing into the house after frosty hikes from school, to smell the sweet, spicy fragrance of Mother's Christmas cookies . . . Dad's mysterious trips to town to bring back those wonderful, rustly packages he hid in the closet!

Sunday afternoon excursions to the woods to pick mistletoe, and cedar boughs to decorate the parlor . . . or chinaberry pods to make a string of beads for a friend!

Carefully saving our pennies for that very special gift . . . lingering hours spent peering into store windows overflowing with the magic temptations of Christmas . . . the heart-twisting decision between the beautiful brooch, or the warm gloves Mother needed . . . the longing looks at that beautiful doll with the real hair!

"Stringing night" . . . the tantalizing aroma of Mother's freshly-popped corn, which couldn't be eaten until enough had been strung for the tree . . . singing carols while hanging ornaments on the tree, mistletoe on chandeliers, bells on the doors . . . heaping bowls of nuts, peppermint sticks, twisted candy, big round oranges, shiny red apples . . . cracking nuts on a flatiron!

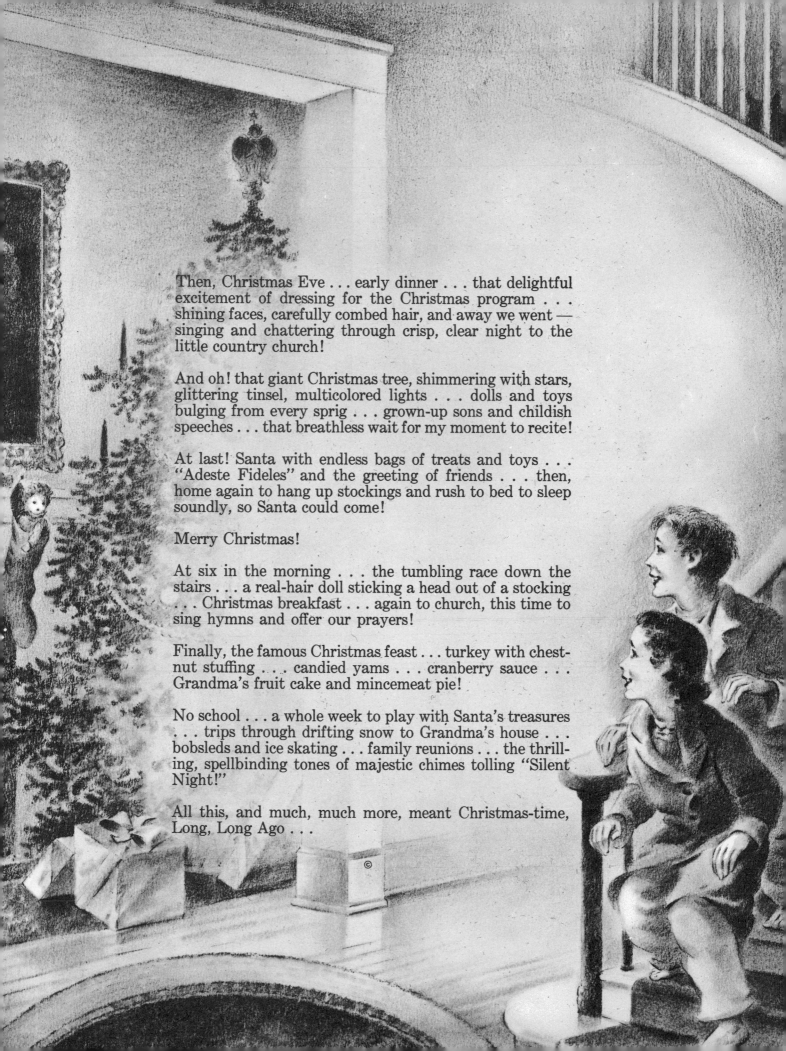

Then, Christmas Eve . . . early dinner . . . that delightful excitement of dressing for the Christmas program . . . shining faces, carefully combed hair, and away we went — singing and chattering through crisp, clear night to the little country church!

And oh! that giant Christmas tree, shimmering with stars, glittering tinsel, multicolored lights . . . dolls and toys bulging from every sprig . . . grown-up sons and childish speeches . . . that breathless wait for my moment to recite!

At last! Santa with endless bags of treats and toys . . . "Adeste Fideles" and the greeting of friends . . . then, home again to hang up stockings and rush to bed to sleep soundly, so Santa could come!

Merry Christmas!

At six in the morning . . . the tumbling race down the stairs . . . a real-hair doll sticking a head out of a stocking . . . Christmas breakfast . . . again to church, this time to sing hymns and offer our prayers!

Finally, the famous Christmas feast . . . turkey with chestnut stuffing . . . candied yams . . . cranberry sauce . . . Grandma's fruit cake and mincemeat pie!

No school . . . a whole week to play with Santa's treasures . . . trips through drifting snow to Grandma's house . . . bobsleds and ice skating . . . family reunions . . . the thrilling, spellbinding tones of majestic chimes tolling "Silent Night!"

All this, and much, much more, meant Christmas-time, Long, Long Ago . . .

Christmas Is Remembering.....

Hilda Butler Farr

Christmas is remembering...
The road to Santa Claus,
The blessed time of childhood
That meant so much...because
It held the tinseled magic
Of fairyland array,
When all the world was laughter —
And life was only play.

Christmas is remembering...
A tree ablaze with light,
The family gathered closely
And knowing deep delight.

Exchanging gifts and sharing,
The gaiety and song
That star the festive season —
Each time it comes along.

Christmas is remembering...
Our friends who're far and near,
By giving and receiving...
A season always dear.

The mistletoe and holly,
As scarlet tapers glow,
The Christ Child in a manger —
So very long ago.

©

Backward, turn backward, O Time in your flight;
Make me a child again just for tonight.

Elizabeth Akers Allen
(1832-1911)

Edgar A. Guest

He little knew the sorrow
That was in his vacant chair;
He never guessed they'd miss him,
Or he'd surely have been there;
He couldn't see his mother
Or the lump that filled her throat,
Or the tears that started falling
As she read his hasty note;
And he couldn't see his father,
Sitting sorrowful and dumb,
Or he never would have written
That he thought he couldn't come.

He little knew the gladness
That his presence would have made,
And the joy it would have given,
Or he never would have stayed.
He didn't know how hungry
The little mother had grown
Once again to see her baby
And to claim him for her own.
He didn't guess the meaning
Of his visit Christmas Day
Or he never would have written
That he couldn't get away.

He couldn't see the fading
Of the cheeks that once were pink,
And the silver in the tresses;
And he didn't stop to think
How the years are passing swiftly,
And next Christmas it might be
There would be no home to visit
And no mother dear to see.
He didn't think about it —
I'll not say he didn't care,
He was heedless and forgetful
Or he'd surely have been there.

Are you going home for Christmas?
Have you written you'll be there?
Going home to kiss the mother
And to show her that you care?
Going home to greet the father
In a way to make him glad?
If you're not I hope there'll never
Come a time you'll wish you had.
Just sit down and write a letter —
It will make their heart strings hum,
With a tune of perfect gladness —
If you'll tell them that you'll come.

*Going Home
for
Christmas*

When Christmas Comes

Edwin Osgood Grover

Christmas again! With its peace, and good will, and wonder! How our spirit swells, and our kindliness multiplies and increases in value as the Day of Days draws near! The touch of human hand thrills us; we are not ashamed to be good ... to be kind ... to be loving. For this little pause out of the long, selfish year we are glad to be ourselves.

We give freely of our love and kindness; we offer our labor without price; we speak precious words that are rarer far than rubies. Once more we take courage and let our heart have its way, and life laughs and is glad.

When Christmas comes the world suddenly grows better, sin is less alluring, and Heaven is nearer. Perhaps, if we tried ... who knows ... we might carry with us throughout the year, the joy of Christmas.

©

"Be It Ever So Humble..."

Ethel G. Hokser

Home is where the heart is . . . where love and reverence reign . . . where there is a spirit of harmony and a feeling of safe security . . . where there is neither selfishness, nor bickering, nor discord, nor a lack of respect . . . where the great virtues of sympathy, kindness, and gentleness are practiced every hour of every day . . . where the child learns to know, to understand, and to practice only that which is right . . . where we come together to find the joy and the happiness of the companionship of family and the fellowship of friends and to say grace at mealtime and a prayer at close of day.

And at this Yuletide season let us be reminded that all this had its beginning with the birth of the Christ-Child in the most humble of places. Just as that first humble Christian home radiated love, faith, hope and charity, let us likewise carry these virtues in our hearts . . . but above all let us be humble and forgiving not just for an hour or a day, but for every day . . . then and only then shall there be "Peace on earth, good will among men."

Snow on Christmas Eve

Annette May Jones

The snow fell fast on Christmas Eve,
Flakes whirling round and round
Yet making not a sound,
And what grand magic they did weave,
As earth became a wonderland.

After the falling of the snow
A freezing wind swept down
On countryside and town —
Night long it did not cease to blow
Until a spread of sleet was laid.

When morning dawned the sun shone bright,
And then rare beauty gleamed
Wherever sunlight beamed,
For countless gems flashed in the light —
The jewels of the snow and ice.

The crystal light shone through the trees
From dainty pearls that hung
With great tenacity — and these
Were lovelier than mere words can portray.

The glistening white lay on the ground
Like frosting on a cake
That artful hands might make,
And through the wintry air a sound
Was heard — the elfin horns of frost.

Then Christmas bells began to ring
And petty cares took flight,
All hearts became so light
You might have heard the angels sing —
For tender Love ruled everywhere.

Time Long Ago

Ora Pate Stewart

Time long ago, on an Indian Summer night,
When the harvest was put away,
And children were snuggled in feather beds
At close of a busy day —

Then Father would sit at the open hearth
And fashion with knife and scroll
A hobby horse, or a sturdy sled,
Or maybe a wooden doll —
While Mother maneuvered the crochet hook,
Or schemed with the calico . . .
And fascinators and pinafores
Danced polkas in a row.

It isn't that world economy
Has untethered his silver wings . . .
But that, atticked away in a cob-webbed age,
Lies the pleasure of making things.

©

A Boy at Christmas

Edgar A. Guest

If I could have my wish tonight,
  it would not be for wealth or fame;
It would not be for some delight
  that men who live in luxury claim,
But it would be that I might rise
  at three or four a.m. to see,
With eager, happy, boyish eyes,
  my presents on the Christmas tree.
Throughout this world there is no joy,
  I know now I am growing gray,
So rich as being just a boy,
  a little boy on Christmas Day.

I'd like once more to stand and gaze
  enraptured on a tinseled tree,
With eyes that know just how to blaze,
  a heart still tuned to ecstasy;
I'd like to feel the old delight,
  the surging thrills within me come:
To love a thing with all my might,
  to grasp the pleasure of a drum;
To know the meaning of a toy —
  a meaning lost to minds blase;
To be just once again a boy,
  a little boy on Christmas Day.

I'd like to see a pair of skates
  the way they looked to me back then,
Before I'd turned from boyhood's gates
  and marched into the world of men;
I'd like to see a jackknife, too,
  with those same eager, dancing eyes
That couldn't fault or blemish view;
  I'd like to feel the same surprise,
The pleasure, free from all alloy,
  that has forever passed away,
When I was just a little boy
  and had my faith in Christmas Day.

Oh, little, laughing, roguish lad,
  the king that rules across the sea
Would give his scepter if he had
  such joy as now belongs to thee!
And beards of gray would give their gold,
  and all the honors they possess,
Once more within their grasp to hold
  thy present fee for happiness.
Earth sends no greater, surer joy —
  as thou, too soon, shall also say —
Than that of him who is a boy,
  a little boy on Christmas Day.

"Merry Christmas!"

Mary H. Beam

No words, new-coined, can ever tell
What this old greeting says so well,
Recalling other Christmas Days
With all their sweet, old-fashioned ways.

* * * *

The childhood dream of sweets and toys
That were the sum of Christmas joys;
Mysterious secrets everywhere,
And snowflakes tumbling through the air.

And then, the greatest thrill of all,
On Christmas Eve, as great and small,
Behind the horses gay with bells,
Glide up the hills and down the dells
To Church!

The church, bedecked with spruce and pine,
The giant tree where candles shine;
The Story of the Child (His bed,
A manger in a cattle shed);
The angels' song, the shepherds' fright;
The Wise Men traveling in the night,
To bring strange gifts from distant lands;
The star-lit path across the sands.
At long, long last, the Christmas "treat"!
Was ever candy half so sweet?

Beside the hearth to hear once more,
The Story, read from Sacred Lore,
And pray the Child to come again
And dwell within the hearts of men.
Around the organ carols sung;
In much ado, the stockings hung.
Then off to bed, for Christmas Day
Was yet some sleep-filled hours away.

* * * *

Though years may come and years may go,
And every sort of wind may blow,
With "Merry Christmas" in the heart,
The joys of Christmas ne'er depart.

I Remember Christmases

Wilma Theodora Hamilton

I remember Christmases in years
   that are long since past,
The warmth and wonder which they held
   is something that will last.
And as the special day draws near,
   I like to meditate
On treasured memories,
   today, considered out of date.
Our homemade Christmases
   were not so glittering, I know,
Nor near as fancy, tinsel-wrapped,
   and yet a certain glow
Enveloped them and lingered
   to charm me through the years;
They draw me back, encircling me,
   as Christmas once more nears.

For weeks before the night of nights,
   we labored hard and long
On a Christmas pageant at the church
   and sang the angel's song;
And all the old familiar carols
   just shook the rafters there,
Hallowed and holy, drifted
   from our little house of prayer.
Walking home, tall stars
   beamed kindly down on us,
And a watching moon would guide
   our steps, pale and luminous.
The Christmas spirit crackled
   through the frosty winter night,
And golden windows beckoned us
   with lamp and warm firelight.

Our Christmas decorations
   were made by one and all —
A cardboard star with tinfoil
   to top the tree so tall;
Santa made of red art paper
   to hang upon the door;

And bowls of popcorn with the strings
    spread across the floor.
O such happy times we had
    hiding gifts away —
"Do not open," on each one,
    "Not till Christmas Day."
Tied with love and laughter
    though the price tag wasn't high;
The gifts we gave each other then,
    money could not buy.

Climbing trees for mistletoe,
    making wreaths of holly,
Snatch of song reminding us,
    "tis the season to be jolly";
Tramping through the winter woods
    for our Christmas tree,
(Scent of pine and cedar
    sharp as it could be).
Chopping down the biggest one
    that our house could hold,
Hurrying home through early dusk,
    growing bitter cold.
Apples polished, cranberries strung
    before a glowing fire;
Kitchen sending out such smells
    whetting our desire.

I remember Christmases in years
    that are long since gone;
All this excitement in the air,
    with Christmas coming on,
Brings back a flood of memories
    I welcome in my heart,
Grown dearer with each passing year,
    with loved ones far apart.
When Christmas candles light the dark
    and trees with tinsel drip,
And a star in the east hangs low
    and bright, then I must take a trip
Back to my childhood when I hung
    my stocking with great care,
And Santa filled it in the night
    and left it waiting there.

A Child Again

William A. Washburn

Most of all the time I like to think
That all my childish ways
Are but mementos of the past:
Forgotten yesterdays;
But once a year, at Christmastime,
There comes a sudden change,
The years don't seem to count for much —
I'm just a child again.

The decorated Christmas tree
Adorned with angel's hair;
A dad and mother, hearts made light,
With all their children there;
Some simple gifts that speak of love,
Each a surprise to bring,
When all these things come to my mind —
I'm just a child again.

We've all been taught that Christmastime
Is just for girls and boys —
The little tots who like to play
With dolls, and blocks, and toys —
Perhaps it is, but when gay hearts
The Christmas carols sing,
The years don't mean a thing to me —
I'm just a child again.

©

Yes, I Remember Well —

Christmas
When I Was a Little Girl

It seems only yesterday - when I was a little girl - just like you - and when it was Christmas time at our house - yes, my dear - only yesterday.

We lived in a small town - Daddy owned the general store - it seemed that almost everyone lived in small towns - because only yesterday - most towns were small.

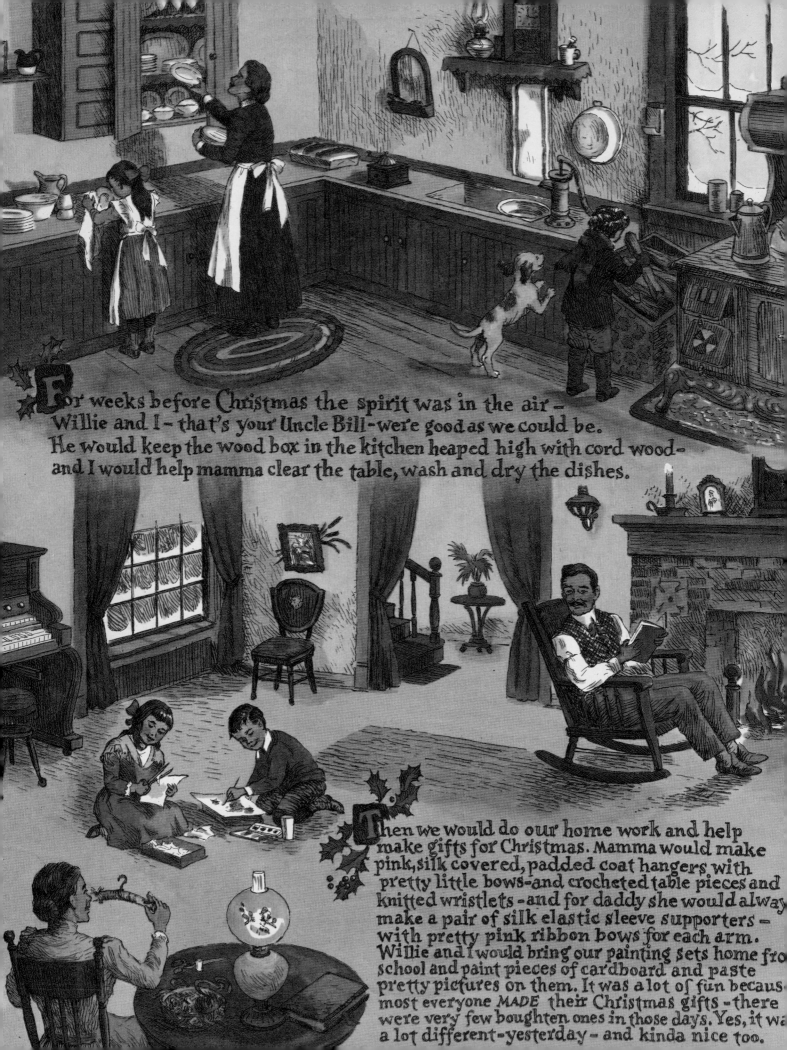

For weeks before Christmas the spirit was in the air —
Willie and I — that's your Uncle Bill — were good as we could be.
He would keep the wood box in the kitchen heaped high with cord wood —
and I would help mamma clear the table, wash and dry the dishes.

Then we would do our home work and help
make gifts for Christmas. Mamma would make
pink, silk covered, padded coat hangers with
pretty little bows — and crocheted table pieces and
knitted wristlets — and for daddy she would always
make a pair of silk elastic sleeve supporters —
with pretty pink ribbon bows for each arm.
Willie and I would bring our painting sets home from
school and paint pieces of cardboard and paste
pretty pictures on them. It was a lot of fun because
most everyone MADE their Christmas gifts — there
were very few boughten ones in those days. Yes, it was
a lot different — yesterday — and kinda nice too.

When the clock on the mantel would strike half past eight - Willie and I were hustled off to bed. Just before we went upstairs, daddy would read to us about the first Christmas - from St. Luke and Matthew - in the bible. Then we'd quickly say our prayers at mamma's knee - and then go to bed.

hey were big fluffy beds - with feather ticks and feather comforters. On real cold nights, Mamma would wrap a hot sad iron in a piece of flannel and would put it in our bed at our feet and soon we would be sound asleep - dreaming dreams about Christmas.

Even on our way to school there was happy talk about Christmas doings at everyone's house - and the gifts that were being made. In school - for weeks before - we would sing all the old Christmas carols and recite Christmas poems - getting ready for the Christmas exercises.

And at Sunday school it was the same thing. We would sing all the beautiful Christmas songs - and rehearse the Story of the Nativity over and over again. Willie was a shepherd - and one year I played the part of Mary - I will never forget the warm glowing feeling - and the tears in mamma's eyes - when I tenderly showed my doll in the crib to the Shepherds.

A few days before Christmas, daddy would let Willie and me go with him to pick out our tree for Christmas. We didn't buy them on the corner those days - we would go out in the woods and chop one down.

Christmas Eve came at last - with big white snow flakes in the air - and the bells on the sleighs would jingle jingle - you could hear them for miles in the clear cold air.

Right after supper we all bundled up and walked to church services. Christmas was never so beautiful - everyone so gay and happy - the church was aglow with candles and Christmas decorations - and there was the manger setting - where our play "The Story of the Nativity" would be presented.

Oh!—Christmas Eve was a happy, busy time.
When we returned home from church—we hung
our stockings over the fireplace—placed a couple
pieces of brown sugar on a plate for Santa's
reindeer and a piece of cake for Santa—
said a very special prayer that night—
and in our excitement to go to bed
—we forgot our hot iron.

We quivered with excitement—as we listened with strained ears
to all the unusual sounds we heard that night. We KNEW we
could hear Santa's reindeer on the roof—and Santa talking in
muffled tones to his brownies who were helping him.
Finally we drifted off to slumberland—and when we heard daddy
shake the grates in the kitchen stove—we knew Christmas
morning was here at last!

We raced downstairs – still in our flannel nightgowns – and – lo and behold! – the most wonderful – beautiful – thrilling sight in our lives – was our gorgeous tree all trimmed with colored paper chains – stringed popcorn – and shining doodads – and a big glistening star right on top – with a million colored candles carefully clipped at the end of every branch –

And Willie was busy admiring his brand new pair of clamp-on skates – a new knit stocking cap – mittens – a magic lantern – and a brand new pair of brown leather boots with bright copper toes.

And there beneath the tree was the very same little cast iron cooking stove I had looked at in the store window so many times. It was just like mamma's – And there was a real store bought girl's sled with swan's head runners – bright red mittens – a green scarf – new stockings – and my oh my – a brand new pair of high buttoned shiny patent leather shoes for Sunday.

God Bless

And our stockings — Santa was certainly
wonderful to us — in the toe of each stocking
was a real orange — and nuts and apples —
and a tin horn — and some hard ribbon candy —
and some peppermint canes —
It was wonderful!

About eleven o'clock dad would hitch up the two mares to the sleigh and we would drive out to the farm for Christmas dinner with Grandma and Grandpa - all of our kin folks were there - Grandma had been preparing the dinner for days. We don't seem to have those happy family get togethers any more - and it's a shame - we are missing a lot.

After dinner we skated on the pond -

and tried out our new sleds

we sang songs

and played dominoes and looked at the stereoscope pictures - and we were generally so tuckered out that we fell sound asleep in the sleigh on the way home -

Yes - I remember well - Christmas when I was a little girl - they were happy, happy days - and it seems only yesterday.

A Prayer
at Christmas

Give us the faith of innocent children, that we may look forward with hope in our hearts, to the dawn of happy tomorrows.

Reawaken the thought that our most cherished desires will be realized, the things closest to our hearts—that we may come to an appreciation of the limitless joys and bountiful rewards of Patience, Charity and Sacrifice.

Above all, endow us with the spirit of courage, that we may face the perplexities of a troubled world without flinching, imbued with the child=like faith which envisions the beautiful and inspiring things of life . . . and restore the happy hours and experiences so many of us foolishly believe are lost forever.

Give us faith in ourselves and faith in our fellow man . . . then, the treasures and beauties of life that make man happy will spring from an inexhaustible source.

And at Christmas, when the hearts of the world swell in joyous celebration, let us cast aside the pretense of sturdy men and live, if only for a day, in the hope and joy we knew as children.

Our sincere thanks
to the unknown author.

There'll Always Be Christmas...

Edna Jaques

There'll always be Christmas
  . . as long as a light
Glows in the window
  to guide folks at night,
As long as a star
  in the heavens above,
Keeps shining down . . .
  there'll be Christmas and love.

There'll always be Christmas . . .
  as long as a tree
Grows on a hilltop . . .
  as long as the sea
Breaks into foam
  on a white pebbled beach,
As long as there's laughter
  and beautiful speech.

There'll always be Christmas . . .
    as long as a street
Gives back the echo
    of homeward bound feet,
And children with mittens
    and warm winter clothes
Have bright eyes that sparkle
    and cheeks like a rose.

There'll always be Christmas . . .
    with holly and snow,
And church bells that ring
    in the valley below,
Shop windows lighted
    and doorways ajar,
And over the housetops
    the glint of a star.

The cavernous length
    of a stocking to fill,
A wreath on the window . . .
    a light on a hill,
The song of the angels . . .
    and over again
The beautiful message . . .
    Good will among men.

©

64 nostalgic pages
size 8 ½ by 11 inches

$150
per copy
cellophaned
HARD BOUND cover

80 inspiring pages
size 8 ½ by 11 inches

$150
per copy
cellophaned
HARD BOUND cover

CHRISTMAS MEMORY LANE

Walk along the lane to Christmas of yesteryear. Happy days of the long ago recall the memory-laden Christmases of days gone by. The excitement, the anticipation, the thrill of "Christmas in the air", that you experienced are portrayed in poetry, prose and colorful art reproductions. A joy to read, a book to treasure.

RELIGIOUS CHRISTMAS STORIES FOR CHILDREN

A most interesting book that will bring happiness to all young children during the Christmas season. A lovely collection of Christmas stories — some new, some your very own long-time favorites. A cherished book for children of all ages — with stories that will be remembered all of their lives.

24 colorful pages
size 8 ½ by
11 inches

$150
per copy
cellophaned
HARD BOUND cover

48 magnificent
pages
size 8 ½ by
11 inches

$150
per copy
cellophaned
HARD BOUND cover

THE NIGHT BEFORE CHRISTMAS

The wonderful old, old story by Clement C. Moore — that has fascinated and thrilled and sparked the dreams of children for generations. Brand new — from cover to cover — with twenty-four full page color paintings made especially for this issue by Donald Mills. A book that will bring exciting happiness to every child.

THUS IT IS WRITTEN

Embellished and inscribed on parchment, like ancient manuscripts, these exquisitely beautiful engrossments have thrilled many thousands as they have been exhibited throughout the entire country. Each scroll, its designs, symbols, colors and forms and meanings are described to you. We are proud to present them in book form for your inspiration.

72 exquisite pages
size 8 ½ by 11 inches

$**1** 50
per copy

cellophaned
HARD BOUND cover

96 interesting pages
size 8 ½ by 11 inches

$**1** 50
per copy

cellophaned
HARD BOUND cover

THE TRUE RELIGIOUS CHRISTMAS

A colorful book dedicated to the true reverent spirit of the Christmas season. Poems and prose, beautiful full color art reproductions, lend themselves to a thoughtful presentation of inspiration and devotion. The happy hours of pleasure make this book a delightful reading experience as each page tells of the religious significance of this Holy Season.

THE HAPPY CHRISTMAS STORY BOOK

Many, many hours of childhood happiness packed into this new BIG book of Christmas st — filled with the old, old favorites — and new too. These are stories to be read aloud. Each s is beautifully and artistically illustrated with cially prepared art. A children's gift that wi read, enjoyed and cherished for years to come.

48 melodious pages
size 8 ½ by 11 inches

$**1** 50
per copy

cellophaned
HARD BOUND cover

48 colorful pages
size 8 ½ by 11 inches

$**1** 50
per copy

cellophaned
HARD BOUND cover

CHRISTMAS CAROLS THAT NEVER GROW OLD

Favorite Christmas hymns and carols are reproduced in an artistic and colorful way to bring a tradition of song to your home this year. The melodious carols will add to the joy of Christmas and will bring back glowing memories in song of Christmases past. Make Christmas a season of song.

A TREASURE OF CHRISTMAS RELIGIOUS AR

A revised and enlarged book — more beautiful ever — each colorful art masterpiece brings to the famous-well-loved-Christmas religious art — the Old Masters, as well as by the talented temporary artists. You will acclaim each exqu page *"Beautiful Enough to Frame"*.

IDEALS PUBLISHING CO.
Milwaukee, Wis. © 1965
America's most beautiful and wholesome publications

Your Personal Order

Important — Items checked here will be sent directly to you at the address below. Your ZIP code is an important part of your address — it insures rapid accurate handling of your mail

YOUR NAME _____

ADDRESS _____

CITY _____

STATE _____   ( ) ZIP CODE _____

ITEM		QUANTITY	AMOUNT
CHRISTMAS MEMORY LANE	@ $1.50		
RELIGIOUS CHRISTMAS STORIES FOR CHILDREN	@ $1.50		
THE NIGHT BEFORE CHRISTMAS	@ $1.50		
THUS IT IS WRITTEN	@ $1.50		
THE TRUE RELIGIOUS CHRISTMAS	@ $1.50		
THE HAPPY CHRISTMAS STORY BOOK	@ $1.50		
CHRISTMAS CAROLS THAT NEVER GROW OLD	@ $1.50		
A TREASURE OF CHRISTMAS RELIGIOUS ART	@ $1.50		
DICKENS' CHRISTMAS CAROL	@ $1.50		
CHRISTMAS STORIES THAT NEVER GROW OLD	@ $1.50		
CHRISTMAS AROUND THE WORLD	@ $1.50		
JOLLY OLD SANTA CLAUS	@ $1.50		
WE SAY OUR PRAYERS	@ $1.50		
FRIENDSHIP	@ $1.50		
WORDS ETERNAL	@ $1.50		
JUST BEFORE BED TIME	@ $1.50		
THE CIRCUS	@ $1.50		
FLAGS OF AMERICA	@ $1.50		
IDEALS SCRAP BOOK	@ $1.50		
	TOTAL		

Your Gift Order

To: _____

ADDRESS _____

CITY _____

STATE _____   ( ) ZIP CODE _____

from _____

ITEM		QUANTITY	AMOUNT
CHRISTMAS MEMORY LANE	@ $1.50		
RELIGIOUS CHRISTMAS STORIES FOR CHILDREN	@ $1.50		
THE NIGHT BEFORE CHRISTMAS	@ $1.50		
THUS IT IS WRITTEN	@ $1.50		
THE TRUE RELIGIOUS CHRISTMAS	@ $1.50		
THE HAPPY CHRISTMAS STORY BOOK	@ $1.50		
CHRISTMAS CAROLS THAT NEVER GROW OLD	@ $1.50		
A TREASURE OF CHRISTMAS RELIGIOUS ART	@ $1.50		
DICKENS' CHRISTMAS CAROL	@ $1.50		
CHRISTMAS STORIES THAT NEVER GROW OLD	@ $1.50		
CHRISTMAS AROUND THE WORLD	@ $1.50		
JOLLY OLD SANTA CLAUS	@ $1.50		
WE SAY OUR PRAYERS	@ $1.50		
FRIENDSHIP	@ $1.50		
WORDS ETERNAL	@ $1.50		
JUST BEFORE BED TIME	@ $1.50		
THE CIRCUS	@ $1.50		
FLAGS OF AMERICA	@ $1.50		
IDEALS SCRAP BOOK	@ $1.50		
	TOTAL		

Your Book Dealer or Book Department can supply — or obtain these books for you!

THE CIRCUS

Clowns, trapeze artists, animal trainers, elephants and all the other thrilling acts — they're all here in one enchanting book.

Imagine yourself in the best seat under the big top with the show about to begin — the ringmaster is introducing the first stupendous, super-colossal attraction...

Relive this enjoyable moment and all the wonderful events that make up a "day at the circus". These cherished memories will come to life again with your first glimpse of "THE CIRCUS".

68 colorful pages

Colorful pages throughout — reproductions of the finest in circus art — pictures and paintings of most of your favorites — poems and articles that will please the "young in heart" — this is "THE CIRCUS".

Unique in its presentation — "THE CIRCUS" is a truly authentic look at the tradition-steeped world that we all at one time wished to adopt for our career. Order your copy today and...

Send additional copies to your friends, relatives and that "little someone special" whose eyes you know will light up with wonder and delight at these beautiful pages.

$1.50
per copy

cellophaned
HARD BOUND cover

Scrap Book

The new "IDEALS SCRAP BOOK" has been specially prepared to acquaint our new readers with the type and quality of inspiring poetry, prose, photographs, art that are featured in EVERY issue of IDEALS.

Each issue of IDEALS features one principal theme — some of the subjects have included CHRISTMAS — EASTER — FAMILY — THANKSGIVING — VACATION — INSPIRATION.

IDEALS SCRAP BOOKS contain pages of colorful beauty-poetry and prose depicting the glorious seasons of the year — Spring and Easter — Summer and Vacation — Autumn and Harvest — Winter and Christmas — true wholesome, old-fashioned nostalgic remembrances of the happy days of long ago.

Order your IDEALS SCRAP BOOKS TODAY — and keep a supply on hand of these lovely gift books.

These issues will meet your exacting demands for a quality gift to present for special HOLIDAYS — BIRTHDAYS — GRADUATIONS — ANNIVERSARIES and other important days.

96 interesting pages

$1.50
per copy

cellophaned
HARD BOUND cover

Flags of America

A series of TWENTY rich oil paintings prepared especially for this book by the famous artist GEORGE HINKE tells dramatically the exciting story that surrounds each of the flags that have flown over America.

These paintings portray dramatically the twenty principal flags that have reflected the growth and development of our great country — from the time of the Norsemen until TODAY.

Walk along the historic paths trod by courageous explorers, determined Pilgrims, fearless pioneers, inspired statesmen — and the sturdy men and women who built a new country — founded upon the principles of freedom and justice.

FLAGS OF AMERICA will impart to you — and awaken in your children — the basic principles for which America stands — freedom — justice — opportunity — democracy — accomplishments — and dedication.

You must SEE this exquisite book to appreciate its timeliness, its historic beauty and its importance — especially in these moving times.

48 historic pages

$1.50
per copy

cellophaned
HARD BOUND cover

IDEALS PUBLISHING CO.
Milwaukee, Wis. © 1965

Your Book Dealer or Book Department can supply — or obtain these books for you!